The Official
Ministry of Fun
Joke Book

GW00598796

The Official
Ministry of Fun
Joke Book

The Year's Best Jokes

Norma P. Lamont

Grafton
An Imprint of HarperCollinsPublishers

Grafton
An Imprint of HarperCollins*Publishers*,
77–85 Fulham Palace Road,
Hammersmith, London W6 8JB

A Grafton Original 1992
1 3 5 7 9 8 6 4 2

A catalogue record for this book is
available from the British Library

ISBN 0 586 21860 2

Set in Kaufmann and Frutiger Light

Printed in Great Britain by
HarperCollinsManufacturing Glasgow

*To all fine upstanding members
in the Ministry of Fun.*

Contents

The Celebrity Fun File

A cabinet minister picks up a young actress and they go back to her place. All of a sudden the actress is coming on to him and the minister says, 'Look, I'm very paranoid about AIDS and herpes and all the diseases that are rampant in modern society. Would you mind if we used my big toe instead?' The actress says, 'Why not? I fancy a good toe job,' and proceeds to go down on him.

A couple of weeks later the minister notices that his toe is infected, so he goes to his doctor and says, 'What is wrong with my toe?' The doctor says, 'I can't believe it. The strangest medical things have been happening to me recently. Odd as it sounds, you have oral thrush of the toe.' And the minister says, 'My God! I can't believe it!' And the doctor says, 'Well, that's not too bad. Last week I had a woman in here with athlete's foot of the gums!'

David Mellor was at home in bed with his wife when there was a terrible thunderstorm. As a great flash of lightning lit up the room, Mellor jumped out of bed shouting, 'I'll buy the negatives!'

What's the similarity between David Mellor and Vinny Jones?

Put them in a Chelsea jersey and they f*** you.

What's worse than being screwed by David Mellor in a Chelsea jersey?

Being screwed by David Mellor in the Arsenal away jersey.

What's the difference between Peter Mellor (ex-Fulham goalkeeper) and David Mellor?

None. They both had trouble keeping clean sheets at Fulham.

What was rusty and chained to the railings outside Lambeth Palace?

Terry Waite's bike.

What was Terry Waite's specialist subject on Mastermind?

Lebanese radiators, 1985–91.

Why was the Bishop of Galway sent to Central America?

To take up a missionary position.

What did Donna Rice and Christie McAuliffe have in common?

Both went down on the challenger.

How did Marvin Gaye die?

He heard it through the carbine.

It has just been disclosed that Frank Bough wants to commentate at the next Olympics. He's heard they're sponsored by Coke.

A young Irish lad goes into the confessional where the Bishop of Galway is presiding, and says, 'Bless me, Father, for I have sinned.' And the bishop says, 'What are your sins, my son?'

'Well, Father, I've committed adultery.'

'Tell me the name of the young lady, my son.'

'Well, Father, I cannot divulge that information.'

'My boy,' says the bishop, 'was it Mrs Flannagan? I happen to know that she's been putting it about recently.' But the boy says, 'No, Father, it wasn't Mrs Flannagan.'

'Well, was it Mrs O'Reilly? She's a bit of a goer.'

'No, Father, it wasn't Mrs O'Reilly.'

'Well then, sure, it must have been Mrs O'Connor,' says the bishop. 'She never says no to a chap in distress.'

But the boy says, 'No, Father, it wasn't Mrs O'Connor.' So the bishop says, 'But my boy, if you don't tell me, I cannot give you absolution.'

'Well, that's OK, Father,' says the boy. 'You've given me three new leads.'

Why did Indira Gandhi change her deodorant?

Her Right Guard was killing her.

What would you do if you had a gun with two bullets and were locked in a room with Jeremy Beadle, Emlyn Hughes and Saddam Hussein?

Shoot Jeremy Beadle twice.

Jeremy Beadle was enraged at being searched by Customs on his arrival at JFK airport. 'New York is the asshole of the world!' he screamed.

   'Yessir,' said the customs official. 'And I take it you're just passing through?'

What's green, hairy and highly dangerous?

David Bellamy with a machine gun.

Gazza was walking down an Italian street one night, drunk as a skunk, one foot on the kerb and one foot in the gutter. A *carabiniere* stopped him and said, 'I've got to take you in, you're totally drunk.' Gazza said, 'Officer, are you absolutely sure I'm drunk?' The officer said, 'Yes, you're drunk all right.'

'Thank God for that,' said Gazza, 'I thought my knee had gone again.'

Andrew Lloyd Webber was stark naked in front of an open window, doing his morning aerobics. His wife, entering the room, suddenly rushed over and closed the curtains. 'Andrew, you fool!' she shouted. 'I don't want the neighbours to think I love you for your money!'

Martina Navratilova goes to see her gynaecologist. He examines her and says, 'My goodness, this is remarkably well-kept!'

'I know,' says Martina. 'I have a woman in twice a week.'

Did you hear that 'Hurricane' Higgins has been renamed 'Kerrygold'? It's because he's the best butter in Ireland.

Why did Arnold Schwarzenegger and Maria Shriver get married?

They want to breed the first bullet-proof Kennedy.

What's the difference between Russ Abbot and a whoopee cushion?

A whoopee cushion is funny.

What has two hundred legs, no pubic hair and screams?

The front row of a Michael Jackson concert.

Have you heard that Queen have reformed with a new name?

Right Fred's Dead.

The first time ever that Ian Botham arrived at Lord's Cricket Ground he went up to a member and said, 'Excuse me, where are the changing-rooms at?'

The member said, 'Gad, this is Lord's – we don't end a sentence with a preposition.'

'OK,' said Botham, 'where are the changing-rooms at, wanker?'

What are the fastest insects in the world?

Nigel Mansell's head lice.

What's the definition of endless love?

Stevie Wonder and Ray Charles playing tennis!

The first thing Andrew Neill did when he died and got to hell was set up the *Daily Sinner* in competition with heaven's *Guardian Angel*.

One day he ran a nasty piece about God and, quick as a flash, St Peter was on the phone.

'You print a retraction right now,' St Peter demanded, 'or we'll sue.'

'I don't think so,' said Neill confidently. 'I've got all the lawyers.'

Maxwell-mania

What does MIRROR stand for?

Must Invest in Rubber Ring or Raft.

What goes ffssst?

Robert Maxwell's last cigar.

Robert Maxwell was treading water, surrounded by a school of man-eating sharks. They circled him menacingly, ready to make their strike.

'Who's going first?' one shark asked. As is usual for sharks, the leader went up to the fat man and sniffed him before going in for the kill. He returned to the others with a sad expression on his face.

'We can't eat him lads,' he said, 'he's one of us.'

Did you hear that Robert Maxwell bequeathed his body to medical science?

Medical science is contesting the will.

Did you hear, they've finally found out what happened to Robert Maxwell? Apparently he used to invite prostitutes aboard to keep him company when he was cruising, and on this particular night the one he picked was Irish. And like a fool, he asked her to toss him off...

One Derby County supporter was so upset by Robert Maxwell's activities that after a particularly bad match he muscled his way into the directors' box and punched Maxwell square on the jaw.

It is still fondly remembered in the town as the day the fan hit the shit.

Maxwell travelled all the way to Rome and got himself an audience with the Pope. As soon as the two were alone together, he leaned over and whispered, 'Your Holiness, I have an offer I think might interest you. I'm in a position to give you a million pounds if you'll change the wording in the Lord's Prayer from "give us each day our daily bread" to "give us each day our Daily Mirror". Now, what do you say?'

'Absolutely not!' said the shocked Holy Father.

'OK, I understand, it's a big decision,' said Maxwell. 'How about five million pounds?'

'I couldn't contemplate it,' said the Pope.

'Look, I know it's a tough one,' Maxwell insisted. 'Tell you what – I'll go all the way up to fifty million pounds.'

Asking him to leave the room, the Pope called in his cardinals and whispered, 'When is it exactly that our contract with Mother's Pride expires?'

**'How do I stand?' Robert Maxwell asked his doctor.
'I don't know,' said the doctor. 'To me, it's a miracle.'**

Robert Maxwell once had to leave the country before finding out the results of one of his many libel suits. His lawyer promised to let him know the verdict as soon as it was announced. A week later Maxwell received a fax which simply said, 'Justice has triumphed!' Maxwell immediately faxed back his reply: 'Appeal at once!'

The Recession
Fun File

Did you hear that the Bundesbank has agreed to prop up the pound, as long as we agree that the last Geoff Hurst goal wasn't in?

Did you hear about the merger of Xerox and Wurlitzer?

The company will make reproductive organs.

What's the difference between the Bank of England and Stuttgart?

Stuttgart's got more foreign reserves.

The newly deceased arrived in heaven and on being asked his name replied: 'Peter Clowes.'

The angel on the gate looked into his ledger and said, 'I'm sorry, but I can't find an appointment for you. What was your business on earth?

'Head of Barlow Clowes Investments,' Clowes said.

'I'll go and inquire,' said the angel, but when he returned the man was gone. And so were the Pearly Gates.

A prosperous sterling broker and his wife had everything money could buy, until Norman Lamont produced Black Wednesday. He came home with a heavy heart that night and said to his wife, 'You'd better learn to cook, darling, so we can fire the cook. And you'd better learn to clean the house, so we can fire the cleaner.'

His wife thought it over for a few moments and said, 'OK, but you'd better learn to screw, sweetheart, so we can fire the chauffeur.'

How do you make a small fortune at Lloyds?

Start with a large one.

The head of a Lloyds syndicate was giving one of his employees a lecture. 'In business,' he said, 'ethics are very important. For instance, suppose you are running a small business and a customer comes in and settles a £20 account in cash. Just after he's left, you notice he's given you two £20 notes stuck together. Immediately you are faced with a basic ethical question: Should I tell my partner?'

Do you remember Ernest Saunders?

Neither can he.

Did you hear that Ernest Saunders has been made president of the Alzheimer's Society. The first meeting is on … er…

At least it isn't Waldheimer's Disease that he suffers from. That's like Alzheimer's, except that when you get it you forget you were a Nazi...

Ernie Saunders and Gerald Ronson are walking down the road with their lawyer when they encounter a friend. They introduce the two men to each other and, after the introductions, Ernie takes the friend to one side and says, 'You know, this lawyer is brilliant but there's something really weird about him – he's got two assholes.'

'Two assholes?' says the friend. 'How do you know that?'

'Because every time we walk into the Old Bailey the policeman at the door says, "Here comes that brilliant lawyer with the two assholes!" '

What's the difference between a sterling broker and a pigeon?

A pigeon can still leave a deposit on a Porsche.

The Recession Fun File

At an international doctors' convention in Switzerland a conversation was taking place in a restaurant after the day's seminars were over. An Israeli doctor said, 'Medicine in my country is so advanced that we can take a kidney out of one person and put it in another and have him looking for work in six weeks.'

A German doctor said, 'That's nothing. In Germany we can take a lung out of one person and put it in someone else and have him looking for work in six weeks.'

A Russian doctor said, 'In my country, medicine is so advanced that we can take half a heart from one person, put it in another, and have them both looking for work in two weeks.'

The British doctor said, 'That's nothing. We can take an asshole from Kingston, put him in the Cabinet, and have half the country looking for work the next day.'

What's the difference between Siberia and a Rolls Royce showroom?

One is a deserted place rarely visited by human beings and the other is in Russia.

Which is the odd one out: AIDS, herpes, gonorrhoea, a house for sale?

Gonorrhoea. You can get rid of gonorrhoea.

When his small business did worse and worse in the recession, the boss realized that he'd have to lay off one of his two middle managers, despite the fact that Jack and Jill were equally honest and dedicated to their jobs. Unable to decide which to fire, the boss arbitrarily decided that the first to leave his or her desk the next morning would be the one to get the chop.

The next morning found Jill at her desk, rubbing her temples. Asking Jack for some aspirin, she headed for the water machine and that was where the boss caught up with her.

'There's something I've got to tell you, Jill,' he said. 'I'm going to have to lay you or Jack off.'

'Jack off,' she snapped. 'I have a headache.'

Cohen dies, and his wife, being a practical sort of lady, phones the *Daily Telegraph* to have an announcement printed.

'Nothing expensive,' she says. 'Something along the lines of: Cohen's dead.'

'I'm afraid we have a minimum wordage,' says the man at the *Telegraph*. 'The least you can pay for is five words. You might as well add three words and get value for money.'

'All right then,' says Mrs Cohen after a moment's thought, 'change it to: Cohen's dead. Volvo for sale.'

The Royal Fun File

Fergie was sunbathing on the beach at St Tropez, when she was approached by a lifeguard.

'Excuse me, your Highness,' he said, 'but would you mind moving?'

'Why should I?' she asked.

'Because the tide is waiting to come in.'

What does Fergie use that's six inches long and buzzes?

A mobile telephone.

What's big and pink and too hard for Princess Diana in the morning?
The Financial Times.

What does Fergie make for dinner?

Reservations.

'Princess Diana is very pretty.'
  'Yes indeed – a bit like the Venus de Milo.'
  'Venus de Milo?'
  'Yes, beautiful but not all there.'

What's the difference between a Sloane Ranger and a donkey?

One brays, looks like a horse and has pronounced hindquarters, and the other's a donkey.

'I had everything a man could want,' Prince Andrew sobbed on his mother's shoulder. 'Money, position, a lovely home, the love of a beautiful and sexy woman. Then, one day, Fergie walked in and caught me.'

The Royal Fun File

'Fergie, I'm very worried about Charles.'

'Why, what's the matter?'

'He spends a lot of time talking to flowers.'

'I wouldn't worry about that. A lot of people talk to flowers.'

'When they're a design on the wallpaper?'

'Have you ever thought about what you would do if you had the Queen's income?'

'No, but I've often wondered what she would do if she had mine.'

Prince Andrew stood in front of the bedroom mirror, admiring himself as he groomed his hair and adjusted his uniform.

'I wonder how many truly charming and attractive men there are in the world?' he said to Fergie.

'One less than you think,' she muttered.

As Charles and Diana have discovered, when a man and woman marry they become one – the question is, which one?

'Darling,' young Diana whispered to Prince Charles a few days before their wedding, 'will you still love me after we're married?'

'Probably even more,' he replied. 'I've got a bit of a thing about married women.'

Prince Charles and Princess Anne were walking in the grounds of Balmoral, earnestly discussing the subject of marriage.

'You know,' said Charles, 'I never really knew the meaning of happiness until I got married.'

'Yes,' said Anne sadly, 'and then it's too late.'

Princess Anne decided to help Save The Children by holding a fête in the grounds of Gatcombe House. She ran the white elephant stall herself, and invited members of the Royal family to bring along something they had no use for. Edward brought his Royal Marines uniform, the Queen brought an Income Tax demand and the Queen Mother brought a losing betting slip. Diana and Fergie brought their husbands.

The day before he was married, Prince Charles was taken to one side by his father.

'Now, my lad,' said Prince Philip. 'You'll look back on today as the happiest day of your life.'

'But it's tomorrow that I get married,' said Prince Charles.

'I know, son, I know.'

The Queen's television broke down the other day so she went down to the TV shop to buy another one. 'What make do you want?' asked the assistant.

'One doesn't particularly mind,' said the Queen, 'as long as it's not a Philips or a Ferguson.'

The Queen and Princess Diana are driving a Range Rover through Windsor Great Park one day when an armed robber jumps out of the bushes, motions them to a halt and demands all their money and jewels.

'I'm sorry, young man,' says the Queen, 'but as you can see, I have no money.'

'Yah, me too. I'm awfully sorry,' says the Princess, 'but as you can see, I have no jewels.'

Muttering angrily, the robber contents himself with stealing the car, and drives off into the distance.

'I hope you don't mind my asking, ma'am,' says Princess Diana, 'but when we set out you had at least five hundred pounds with you. Where did you manage to hide it?'

'One concealed it in one's special female place,' replied the Queen.

'Yah, me too,' blushed Princess Diana. 'That's where I hid my jewels.'

'You know,' said the Queen as they walked on, 'it's a pity we didn't have Fergie with us.'

'Why's that?' asked the Princess.

'Because then we could have saved the Range Rover.'

Prince Charles calls up his lawyer and tells him he is suing for divorce. 'On what grounds?' the lawyer asks.

'Can you believe it?' the prince splutters angrily. 'My wife says I'm a lousy lover!'

'That's why you're suing?' asked the lawyer.

'Of course not. I'm suing because she knows the difference.'

Why does Fergie wear a tight bra?

One yank and it's off.

To celebrate the victory of the Yes vote in the French referendum, John Major took the entire cabinet out to dinner at the smartest French restaurant in London.

'What would you like for your main course?' the waiter asked him.

'Steak,' he replied.

'*Certainement*, the steak for *monsieur*,' said the waiter. 'And what about the vegetables?'

'Oh, steak for them as well, please.'

A satirical magazine printed an article in which it was stated that half of John Major's cabinet were morons. Furious, he telephoned the editor and demanded that the magazine publish an immediate retraction. In the next issue the publishers apologized, and said that half of John Major's cabinet were not morons.

What did Paddy Ashdown say when he was accused of being wishy-washy?

'Maybe I am, maybe I'm not.'

What's good news for John Smith?

John Major opening his mouth.

The Education Secretary, John Patten, died and knocked on the gates of heaven. To his surprise the gates were opened not by St Peter but by the devil.

'Don't be surprised,' said the devil, 'we've gone comprehensive.'

Douglas Hurd just cannot understand the continuing strife in the Middle East. He thinks that the Arabs and the Jews should learn to live in peace like all good Christians.

Peter Brooke used to complain that every time he found a solution to the Irish question, the Irish changed the question.

'The idea that the British government's environmental policy is built on sand is totally without foundation,' John Major told members of the Earth Summit.

One unkind commentator has remarked that putting Virginia Bottomley in charge of the National Health Service is like putting King Herod on the board of Mothercare.

Virginia Bottomley's favourite joke…
Doctor to patient: 'Are you on the NHS or would you like an anaesthetic?'

Why is Cecil Parkinson like a piece of furniture from MFI?

One screw in the wrong place and the whole cabinet fell apart.

Treasury first aid instructor to employee: 'What telephone number would you dial if the Chancellor had a heart attack?'

Employee: '998.'

After all their years together, John Major is finally developing an attachment for Norman Lamont. It fits over his mouth.

John Major reports that this has been an average year for unemployment. That means that it is a good deal worse than last year, and a good deal better than next year.

Three doctors were sitting around drinking coffee one morning after an early session of operations.

'I reckon the operation I performed this morning was the easiest ever,' said the first doctor.

'Bet mine was easier,' said the second doctor.

'I'd put any money on the fact that mine was the easiest,' said the third.

'I don't know about that,' said the first doctor. 'I operated on a German engineer.'

'I operated on a Japanese electronics expert,' said the second.

'I operated on a British chancellor,' said the third.

'German engineers have got to be the easiest,' said the first doctor. 'You open them up and they have cogs and wheels inside, all neatly numbered. You simply change the part and close them up.'

The second doctor said, 'You're wrong. Japanese electronics experts are definitely the easiest to operate on. They have colour-coded transistors and microchips – you just change a defective component and you're done.'

'You're both wrong,' said the third doctor. 'British chancellors are by far the easiest to operate on. They've only got two moving parts, the mouth and the asshole – and they're interchangeable.'

At the last election, John Major asked the British people to vote for the Conservative Party and sound economic policies. Doesn't he know that it's illegal to vote twice?

What have been the four critical periods for unemployment under John Major's administration?

Spring, summer, autumn and winter.

Over the automatic hand-drier in the Gents at the Labour Party conference someone had written:

Press this button for one-minute speech by John Major

John Major claims to be a self-made man. It's good of him really to take all the blame.

Norman Lamont was attending a cocktail party and was approached by a young man eager to impress him.

'When can we look forward to reading your memoirs, Chancellor?' he asked.

'I shall probably publish my memoirs posthumously,' Lamont replied.

'Oh, how super,' enthused the young man, 'I do hope it's soon.'

The question all the government's enemies are asking is: Where is Guy Fawkes now when his country really needs him?

Actually, Norman Lamont is an awfully modest man. But then, he has an awful lot to be modest about.

According to one observer, Margaret Thatcher was the finest woman prime minister since Neville Chamberlain.

An editor at a posh publishing party in Hammersmith once tried to impress Margaret Thatcher by suggesting that she and Winston Churchill were the only two great politicians of the twentieth century.

'Why drag in Churchill?' she retorted.

Norman Lamont went to his doctor for a check-up. When he had finished his examination the doctor said, 'Mr Lamont, you're as sound as a pound.'

'Oh God,' Lamont exclaimed, 'you mean it's terminal?'

What's the best thing you can get out of John Major's Britain?

A one-way ticket to Tokyo.

At the Labour Party conference, John Smith was asked if he had heard the latest political jokes. 'Heard them?' he said. 'I've appointed them all to the shadow cabinet.'

At the last election, posters appeared of Paddy Ashdown's face with the message 'The Liberal Democrats are the answer.' Underneath one someone had written: 'Then it must have been a bloody silly question!'

What's the definition of the Maastricht Treaty?

The longest suicide note ever written.

What would happen if Norman Lamont was in charge of the Sahara?

Everything would be fine for three years, then there would be an acute shortage of sand.

Norman Lamont doesn't have an IN tray or an OUT tray on his desk. Instead, they say EASY COME and EASY GO.

What's the difference between Thatcherism and Majorism?

Thatcherism was based on the exploitation of one human being by another human being. Majorism is just the opposite.

Why does Shirley Lamont always get on top?

Because Norman can only f*** up.

How many Treasury officials does it take to screw in a light bulb?

Two: one to screw it in and one to screw it up.

What's a synonym for 'incompetent'?

Elected.

What's John Major's favourite colour?

Tartan.

What's David Blunkett's favourite colour?

Corduroy.

John Major was at an international conference when he was introduced to two gentlemen – the Swiss Minister for the Navy and the North Korean Minister for Private Enterprise. 'That's amusing,' he chuckled, 'Switzerland doesn't have any sea boundaries and North Korea doesn't have any private enterprise.'

'What's so funny about that?' asked the North Korean. 'You've got a Minister for Employment.'

The Iraqi Fun File

Did you hear about the new Saddam Hussein doll?

Wind it up and it takes Barbie and Ken as a human shield.

How can you identify an Iraqi soldier?

He's the one with his hands up.

Did you hear, the Irish finally sent their army to the Gulf?
The only trouble is, the Mexicans don't know what to do
with it.

file

_51

Why doesn't anyone in Baghdad bother going to bars any more?

Because they can get bombed at home.

How can you tell a resident of Tel Aviv?

By the Scud-marks in his underpants.

What fast food chain didn't do well in Tel Aviv?

Scud-U-Like.

Why does the new Iraqi navy use glass-bottomed boats?

So they can steer clear of the old Iraqi navy.

Iraqi recruiting poster:

> *Join the army
> and see the next world.*

How many Iraqi arms experts does it take to screw in a light bulb?

Two: one to hold the bulb, and the other to ask the Russian adviser which way to turn it.

What's the difference between the Iraqi army and Ted Kennedy?

Ted Kennedy has at least one confirmed kill.

Did you hear about the Saddam Hussein condom?

It's for men who don't know when to pull out.

During the Gulf War, three allied sailors – an American, an Englishman and an Egyptian – were marooned on a tiny island in the Strait of Hormuz after their boat had struck a mine. Time passed very slowly, until one day a beautiful girl swam ashore, wrapped in a flag which clung to her generous curves. 'She's mine!' yelled the American, pointing to the red, white and blue of the cloth. He tore the flag away, only to reveal a pair of Union Jack panties underneath

'She's mine!' yelled the Brit, 'I claim her for Queen and country.' He elbowed the GI out of the way and tore off her panties.

The Egyptian cleared his throat and declared, 'Ah, the beard of the Prophet...'

What do you call an Iraqi with a sheep under one arm and a goat under the other?

Bisexual.

What's one military idea that never got off the ground?

The Iraqi Air Force.

What's the world's shortest book?

The Wit and Wisdom of Saddam Hussein.

At an Iraqi court martial, the judge read out the indictment, in which the defendant was accused of calling Saddam Hussein a dangerous lunatic. 'The charges against you are threefold,' he stated solemnly. 'First, you have indulged in enemy propaganda. Second, you have slandered our Supreme and Mighty Leader. And third, you have betrayed a military secret.'

What goes 'Hop, skip, jump, *ker-bam*!'?

Kuwaiti children playing in a minefield.

How do you sink the Iraqi navy?

Put it in water.

The Iraqi Fun File

Heard about the ad for Iraqi rifles?

'Never been shot – only dropped once.'

Why do Iraqi pilots learn to fly in half the time?

They don't have to learn how to land.

Did you hear that the allies divided Baghdad into two sections?

Smoking and non-smoking.

Did you hear that Saddam has ordered a thousand septic tanks from Britain?

As soon as the Republican Guard learn how to drive them, they're heading straight back to Kuwait.

What's the new Iraqi army flag?

A white cross on a white background.

Why do they call camels ships of the desert?

Because they're full of Iraqi semen.

By late afternoon it was clear to the Iraqi officer that his platoon was outnumbered and outflanked, and he decided it was time for a little pep talk. 'Keep on fighting, boys,' he said grandly, 'for Saddam and the motherland, until the last shot is fired. Then run.'

He cleared his throat and looked about. 'I'm a little lame, so I'm starting now.'

What do you do when an Iraqi tank is mounting an assault on you?

Shoot the guy pushing it.

Why were so many women soldiers with PMS sent to the Gulf?

They love to pick fights and they retain water for four days.

The International Fun File

What do Ronald Reagan and typewriters have in common?

Semicolons.

Dan Quayle's grasp of Central American affairs is not all it might be. For example, he thinks El Salvador is a Mexican bullfighter – and that manual labour is a Spanish trade unionist.

What do popcorn and Oliver North have in common?

They're both kernels that crack under heat.

Did you hear that Dan Quayle's library got burned down last night? Poor man, he's lost both of his books – and one of them he hadn't even coloured yet.

What did Nancy Reagan say when the press asked her about her sex life with Ronnie?

'Ever tried to shoot pool with a rope?'

George Bush wanted Dan Quayle out of the way during the election campaign so he had him sent on the next NASA mission to the moon, accompanied by a monkey. Both astronauts were issued with a brown envelope. When they landed on the moon's surface the monkey opened his envelope and found his instructions: 'Take seismographic readings every two hours, gather rock core samples from igneous formations and test hourly for atmospheric pressure.' Dan Quayle opened his envelope. It simply said: 'Feed the monkey.'

What did Donna Rice and the presidential election have in common?

Gary Hart pulled out of both of them.

What would be one of the best things for the Americans about electing a woman for president?

They wouldn't have to pay her so much.

A man was walking down a street in Belfast late one night when a shadowy figure, his face obscured by a ski mask, stepped out in front of him. 'Halt!' the masked man called, blocking his path with an automatic rifle. 'Are you Catholic or Protestant?'

The passerby wiped the sweat off his brow. 'Neither,' he replied with a great sigh of relief. 'I'm Jewish.'

The gunman pulled the trigger and blasted his victim to smithereens. Turning away with a grin, he remarked, 'Thanks be to Allah – I must be the luckiest PLO supporter in Ireland tonight.'

The International Fun File

What do you call a pretty girl in Libya?

A tourist.

What's the difference between the Prime Minister of Australia and yoghurt?

Yoghurt has culture.

Staying at the honeymoon hotel were three couples, from America, England and Australia. On the first morning after their weddings they all came down to breakfast. The American man stared into his wife's eyes and said, 'Say, honey, would you please pass me the honey?'

The Englishman stared into his wife's eyes and said, 'Oh, sugar, would you please pass me the sugar?'

The Australian man jabbed his wife in the ribs and said, 'Oi, pass the bacon, you f***ing pig.'

What's fuzzy, smokes and comes in cubes?

Fidel Castro.

What do you call a Falkland islander with a lot of girlfriends?

A shepherd.

How do you get twenty Argentinians in a phone booth?

Let them think they own it.

What would a bad liar say if he were an Israeli government official?

'Arabs are treated just like everybody else ... yeah, that's it.'

What do Japanese men do when they have erections?

Vote.

In South Africa a car carrying two blacks was in collision with a car driven by whites. One black guy was thrown through the windscreen and into the other car. The other black guy was thrown fifty feet into the air and landed in a field. A white South African policeman arrived on the scene and quickly appraised the situation. 'Don't worry, sir,' he said to the white driver. 'I'll book this one for breaking and entering, and his mate for leaving the scene of the crime.'

What do you call a black hitchhiker in Johannesburg?

Stranded.

The body of an ANC official, wrapped in chains, was pulled out of a lake by a South African policeman. The local newspaper reporter asked the chief of police for his thoughts on the case. The chief replied, 'Jesus Christ! Isn't that just like a black boy, stealing more chains than he can swim with?'

What did President de Klerk say after a five-day drinking binge?

'I freed WHO?!'

The Euro Fun File

What do you call a genetic engineering company in Italy?

Genitalia.

How did the Germans capture Poland so easily?

They marched in backwards and said they were leaving.

Why doesn't the Foreign Legion like volunteers who are half-German and half-Italian?

They attack suddenly, then surrender immediately.

It's 1993 and President Mitterrand dies. He goes to heaven but it's not long before he's bored silly and begging St Peter to let him go back to his beloved Paris for one final visit.

'OK,' St Peter finally agrees. 'You've got two hours.'

The president opens his eyes to find himself once again on the Champs Elysées. He immediately finds himself a table at a café and orders a couple of croissants and some coffee. They're both as exquisitely delicious as he remembers them, and he enjoys watching the beautiful women walk by and the Parisians generally going about their business. But all good things must come to an end, and with a sinking heart the president realizes that it's almost time for him to be beamed up.

'*Garçon!*' he calls out, eager to pay before he disappears.

The waiter comes over to the table, and Mitterrand says, '*L'addition, s'il vous plaît.*' Then, wondering about the effects of inflation while he's been away, he adds, 'How much will it be, out of interest?'

The waiter does a quick calculation and says, '*Cinque deutschmarks, monsieur.*'

Why is the Champs Elysées lined with trees?

So the German army can march in the shade.

A Frenchman, an Englishman and a German were boasting about the modes of transport at their disposal. 'I drive a Citroën to work,' said the Frenchman. 'Then at the weekend I drive a Peugeot and when I go abroad I drive a Renault.'

'I drive a Range Rover to work,' said the Englishman. 'Then at the weekend I drive a Rolls Royce and when I go abroad I drive a Jaguar.'

'Well, I drive a BMW to work,' said the German. 'Then at the weekend I drive a Mercedes and when I go abroad I drive a tank.'

What's an innuendo?

An Italian suppository.

'Have you got a new tyre for my Trabant?'

'Yes – that sounds like a good deal.'

What's the difference between heaven and hell?

In heaven the French are the cooks, the Germans are the mechanics, the British are the police, the Italians are the lovers and the Swiss are the bankers.

In hell the French are the mechanics, the Germans are the police, the British are the cooks, the Italians are the bankers and the Swiss are the lovers.

Why does a Trabant have a heated rear windscreen?

To keep your hands warm when pushing it in winter.

What do you call a Norwegian car?

A Fjord.

What are you if you're half Welsh and half Hungarian?

Well Hung.

Did you hear about the Polish ice hockey team?

They drowned during summer training.

How many Poles does it take to go ice-fishing?

Three: one to cut a hole in the ice and two to push the boat through.

Did you hear about the Polish ice-fisherman's wife?

He brought home five hundred pounds of ice and she drowned cooking it.

What do you call an abortion in Czechoslovakia?

A cancelled Czech.

In Britain neo-Nazis are called lager louts. In Germany they're called umlauts.

What's a thousand metres long and eats vegetables?

A Moscow meat queue.

For six years, a Russian has had a car on order from the State factory. Finally one day his doorbell goes and it's a salesman from the factory. 'I have some good news,' he says, 'your car is being delivered in two years' time.'

'That could be a problem,' says the man, 'will it be delivered in the morning or the afternoon?'

'What difference can it possibly make?' asks the salesman. 'A big difference,' says the man. 'I've got the plumber coming in the afternoon.'

What's the Moscow String Quartet?

The Moscow Symphony Orchestra just back from a world tour.

What's the similarity between an Essex girl and Gorbachev?

They both got f***ed by seven men while they were on holiday.

What's the difference between an Essex girl and Gorbachev?

Gorbachev knew their names.

What do gardeners from Chernobyl have?

Incredibly green fingers.

What's the difference between a Croat and a Serb?

A Croat takes the dishes out of the sink before he pisses in it.

What does a Serbian bride get on her wedding night that's long and hard?

A new name.

A Muslim freedom-fighter is captured by the Serbs and taken away for interrogation.

'Which of my eyes is artifical?' asked the torturer. 'If you guess correctly, I'll let you go.'

'The left one,' replied the Muslim without a moment's hesitation.

'How did you know?' asked the Serb.

'It has a more kindly look about it.'

A Serb officer watched in amazement as ten of his heavily armed soldiers were chased by one Muslim villager wielding an ancient sword.

'You cowards!' he screamed. 'Why are you running? There's only one Muslim behind you.'

'That's true, sir,' one of them said as he rushed past. 'But we don't know exactly which one of us he's chasing.'

A Croat, a Serb, an American and a Frenchman were among the passengers in an airliner. Suddenly the pilot announced that the plane was losing altitude due to a terrible mechanical failure.

'Three of you will have to sacrifice yourselves if we are to save the others,' the pilot said. Whereupon the American shouted, 'Long live free America!' and jumped from the plane. Not to be outdone, the Frenchman yelled, 'Long live free France!' and followed the American to his death.

'Long live free Croatia!' shouted the Croat as he grabbed the Serb and threw him out.

How many Italians does it take to screw in a light bulb?

Two: one to screw it in and one to shoot the witnesses.

Kate Adie walks into a shop in Sarajevo and surveys the empty shelves.

'Hmmm … I see you have no bread,' she comments.

'No, we sell meat here – we have no meat,' the shopkeeper replies. 'The shop that has no bread is further down the block.'

What do you get if you cross a Mafioso with an Iraqi?

A hitman who misses.

What do you get if you cross a mafioso with a Glaswegian?

A hitman who makes you an offer you can't understand.

The Final Fun
File

The Essex phenomenon

What's the difference between an Essex girl and Radio Five?

You can't pick up Radio Five after dark.

What's the difference between an Essex girl and Gazza?

Gazza has never scored more than four times in ninety minutes.

How does an Essex girl turn on the light after sex?

She opens the door of the Sierra.

How many Essex girls does it take to screw in a light bulb?

None. Essex girls only screw in Sierras.

What does an Essex girl use for protection during sex?

A bus shelter.

What's an Essex girl's mating call?

'Ooh, I feel really drunk.'

What's the difference between an Essex girl and a supermarket trolley?

A supermarket trolley has a mind of its own.

What's the difference between an Essex girl and the Titanic?

Only 1,490 men went down on the Titanic.

What does an Essex girl have printed in her knickers?

Next.

What's the similarity between the legs of a middle-aged Essex girl and the Beatles?

They haven't been together since the seventies.

What does an Essex girl say after sex?

'Do you really all play for Tottenham Hotspur?'

What does an Essex girl take before sex?

Fourteen large Malibus.

What's an Essex girl's idea of romance?

A lift home afterwards.

What's the difference between an Essex girl and a Rottweiler?

Lip gloss.

What's the difference between an Essex girl and a dictionary?

About 30,000 words.

Essex girl bites back...

How many Essex men does it take to screw in a light bulb?

One. Essex men will screw anything.

How can you tell if an Essex man is sexually excited?

He's breathing.

Why are Essex girl jokes so short?

So Essex men can remember them.

What's an Essex man's idea of helping with the housework?

Lifting his legs so his wife can vacuum.

How can you tell if an Essex man is ambidextrous?

He dribbles from both sides of his mouth.

What's an Essex man's idea of a seven-course meal?

A pizza and a six-pack.

How can you kill an Essex man?

Put a page 3 girl and a pint of lager in front of him and tell him to choose.

What has eight legs and an IQ of forty?

Four Essex men watching football.

Why don't Sloane Rangers enjoy gangbangs?

Too many thank you letters!

What do you call a car accident in Knightsbridge?

A crèche.

What do you call a Sloane Ranger with one 'O' level?

The Princess of Wales.

What do you call a Sloane Ranger at Cambridge University?

Just visiting.

Why is a Sloane Ranger like a Ferrari?

They both cost a fortune and are hard to get into.

What does a Sloane Ranger call her boss?

Daddy

Turning green

What do you call a fruit that's near extinction?

Endangered peaches.

Living near Sellafield affects your short-term memory. The other thing it affects is your short-term memory.

Why did the parrot wear a raincoat?

Because he wanted to be polyunsaturated.

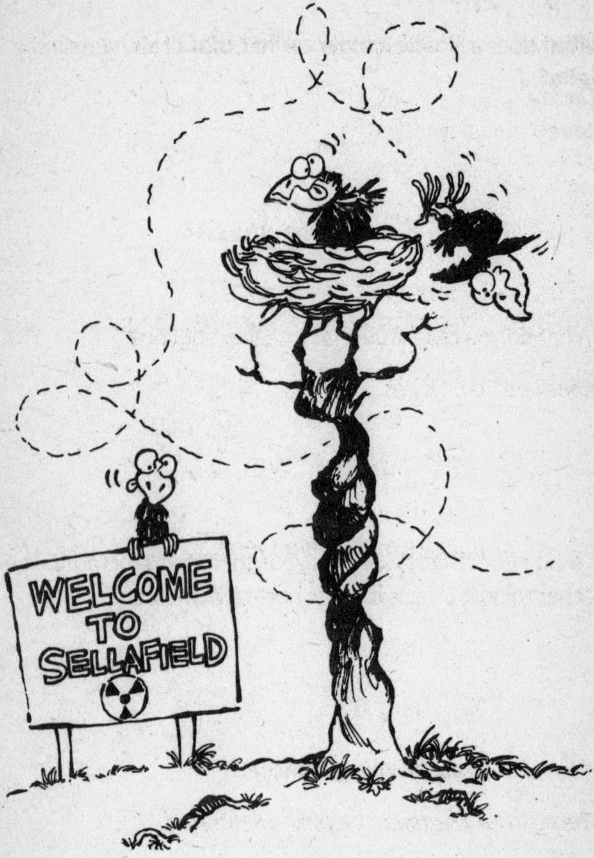
WELCOME
TO
SELLAFIELD

What do you call the crows who build their nests near Sellafield?

Raven lunatics.

Why aren't whales in the North Sea taken seriously?

Because they keep spouting rubbish.

Who campaigns for endangered vegetables?

Green Peas.

How do you spot a nuclear family?

They glow in the dark.

How many Earth Summit delegates does it take to change a light bulb?

Six: one to change the bulb and five to write the environmental impact report.

Why are sheep able to eat grass so quickly in Sellafield?

Because two heads are better than one.

And finally

What's white and slides down the league table?

Aston Vanilla.

What's the most disastrous football team in Britain?

Nottingham Rain Forest.

The Director of Public Prosecutions went up to a young hooker near King's Cross and said, 'What would your mother say if she saw you doing this?'

'She'd kill me,' the girl replied. 'I'm on her corner.'

Anyone can get GCSEs – as long as they can spel.

John Major's private plane caught fire and he had to bail out at twenty thousand feet. He counted to three and pulled his ripcord, but nothing happened. So he counted to three again and pulled the ripcord of his emergency parachute but, again, nothing happened. 'This is it,' he said to himself as he plummeted towards the ground, 'no second term in office for me.'

Then, to his great amazement, he saw that on the ground waiting for him were eleven young Englishmen, all dressed in white, shouting that they would catch him. John Major relaxed as he hurtled towards them. Then, seconds later, to his horror, he realized that they were members of the England cricket team.

What's the first reference to British Rail in the Bible?

'Then God created all creeping things.'

'I'm doing a course in ram-raiding at the University of Wales.'
  'How do you get in?'
  'Well, you have to know how to make a ewe turn – in fact, you have to make its bloody eyes water.'

What's the worst thing about having a heart and lung transplant?

Coughing up someone else's phlegm.

What does DNA stand for?

National Dyslexic Association.

Did you hear about the dyslexic devil worshipper?

He sold his soul to Santa.

What does making love in a canoe have in common with alcohol-free lager?

They're both f***ing close to water.

What did the Irishman say when he was asked what he thought about the Renault 5?

He said they were innocent.

What's the difference between a Rottweiler and a social worker?

It's easier to get your child back from a Rottweiler.

What's got four dog's legs and a child's arm?

A Rottweiler.

What do you call the stinking rich?

The effluent society.

Graffiti seen in Blackpool:

*All this hassle about the Maastricht Bill —
why don't they just pay the bloody thing?*